OPERATION REGAL: THE BERLIN TUNNEL

STUDIES IN CRYPTOGRAPHIC HISTORY

NATIONAL SECURITY AGENCY

NIMBLE BOOKS LLC: THE AI LAB FOR BOOK-LOVERS

~ FRED ZIMMERMAN, EDITOR ~

Humans and AI making books richer, more diverse, and more surprising.

Publishing Information

(c) 2024 Nimble Books LLC
ISBN: 978-1-60888-306-6

AI-generated Keyword Phrases

Operation Regal; Berlin Tunnel; U.S. intelligence community; George Blake; Soviet communications; East German communications; CIA; NSA; Washington REGAL Center; Tunnel.

Publisher's Notes

In a world consumed by information warfare, where the line between truth and deception becomes increasingly blurred, understanding the intricacies of espionage is paramount. The Berlin Tunnel operation, a daring feat of engineering and intelligence gathering that was doomed by forces beyond its control, offers a potent reminder of the lengths nations will go to for strategic advantage—and the costs of failure. As current events unfold on the global stage, reminiscent of the Cold War era, this historical account resonates with renewed relevance, reminding us of the the timeless human drives for power, security, and what can only be called sneakiness.

This annotated edition illustrates the capabilities of the AI Lab for Book-Lovers to add context and ease-of-use to manuscripts. It includes several types of abstracts, building from simplest to more complex: TLDR (one word), ELI5, TLDR (vanilla), Scientific Style, and Action Items; essays to increase viewpoint diversity, such as Grounds for Dissent, Red Team Critique, and MAGA Perspective; and Notable Passages and Nutshell Summaries for each page.

ANNOTATIONS

ABSTRACTS

ANALYSIS BASED ON FULL CONTEXT

These analyses are created by using an large language model (LLM) with a very long input context window, in this case Google Gemini 1.5-pro. The advantage is that the model can use the entirety of the document in its simulated reasoning.

Operation Regal, also known as the Berlin Tunnel, was a top-secret intelligence operation conducted by the United States in the 1950s. Its purpose was to intercept Soviet and East German communications by constructing a tunnel under the Berlin Wall and tapping into underground communication cables. The operation yielded a massive volume of data and provided valuable insights into Soviet military activities, political intentions, and reactions to global events. However, the tunnel was discovered by East German technicians in 1956, leading to a propaganda victory for the Soviets.

Initially hailed as an intelligence triumph, Operation Regal later faced scrutiny regarding the authenticity of the intercepted information. The revelation that British intelligence officer George Blake had been a Soviet double agent during the operation raised concerns about potential disinformation. Blake, present at early planning meetings, likely leaked the tunnel's existence to the Soviets, prompting speculation that they might have manipulated communications to mislead the Americans.

Despite the uncertainty surrounding its ultimate impact, Operation Regal serves as a compelling example of Cold War espionage. The audacious tunnel construction, the enormous volume of intercepted data, and the subsequent involvement of a double agent highlight the high stakes and intricate nature of intelligence operations during this period. Though the operation's true success remains debatable, its legacy continues to intrigue historians and intelligence experts alike.

ANALYSIS BASED ON ABRIDGED CONTENT WINDOWS

These analyzes are created by analyzing portions or summaries of the document, using LLMs with shorter context windows. The advantage is that these models are faster and cheaper.

TLDR (ONE WORD)
Espionage.

EXPLAIN IT TO ME LIKE I'M FIVE YEARS OLD
Operation REGAL was a secret plan where the U.S. tried to listen in on what the Soviet and East German people were saying. They dug a tunnel underground to do this. The Soviets found out about it, but didn't tell the East Germans.

TL;DR (VANILLA)
Operation REGAL, also known as the Berlin Tunnel, was a U.S. intelligence operation designed to intercept Soviet and East German communications. Despite being discovered by the Soviets early on, they did not inform the East Germans of their discovery.

SCIENTIFIC STYLE
Operation REGAL, also known as the Berlin Tunnel, was a covert operation by the U.S. intelligence community aimed at intercepting Soviet and East German communications. Despite initial success, the Soviets, through the betrayal of George Blake, were aware of the operation early on. However, they did not inform the East Germans of their discovery. This operation highlights the intricate and complex nature of Cold War espionage tactics.

ACTION ITEMS
Continue to monitor the situation and assess any potential fallout from the Soviets' knowledge of Operation REGAL.

Review security protocols and procedures to prevent future breaches like the one caused by George Blake.

Consider the implications of the Soviets not informing the East Germans of their discovery and how this may impact future operations in the region.

VIEWPOINTS

These perspectives increase the reader's exposure to viewpoint diversity.

GROUNDS FOR DISSENT

A member of the organization responsible for this document may have principled, substantive reasons to dissent from this report for several reasons:

Lack of transparency: The member may believe that the report does not accurately reflect the level of success of Operation REGAL. They may feel that information is being manipulated or concealed to present a positive image of the operation, when in reality, there were significant flaws or failures that need to be addressed.

Ethical concerns: The member may have ethical concerns about the methods used in Operation REGAL, such as the violation of privacy rights or the potential harm caused to innocent individuals caught up in the surveillance. They may believe that the ends do not justify the means and that a more ethical approach should have been taken.

Strategic implications: The member may have concerns about the strategic implications of the operation being compromised by the Soviets. They may believe that the information obtained could have been used against the U.S. and its allies, leading to potential security risks or diplomatic fallout.

Alternative perspectives: The member may have access to information or perspectives that were not taken into account in the report. They may believe that their dissenting views present a more accurate or nuanced understanding of the situation, and that these perspectives should be considered in any future decision-making processes.

Overall, the member's dissent may stem from a commitment to honesty, integrity, and a desire for the organization to learn from its mistakes and improve its operations in the future.

RED TEAM CRITIQUE

Overall, the document provides a brief overview of Operation Regal, also known as the Berlin Tunnel, a covert operation conducted by the U.S.

PAGE-BY-PAGE SUMMARIES

Notable Passages

BODY-5   "It is an intriguing story, well told. And until the KGB opens its archives, precisely what the Soviets knew and when they knew it remain a mystery."

BODY-6   "Despite its short operational period, REGAL was initially considered a great intelligence success by U.S. officials because of the large volume of information intercepted. There was also an initial feeling of accomplishment in carrying out such an elaborate intelligence scheme literally underneath the feet of the Soviet and East German military."

BODY-7   "Monitoring Berlin's communications would greatly increase the U.S. Soviet-Eastern Europe collection effort. Berlin's telephone and telegraph system resembled a wheel, with two concentric circles spanning East and West Berlin. Switching stations, placed at strategic locations around the circle, directed service to each city sector via lines like the spokes of a wheel."

BODY-8   "Before Harvey laid out his final plane for Washington's approval, an appropriate site had to be selected. The tunnel had to originate in either the U.S. or U.K. zones in Berlin, with a path in range of the targeted cables. The farther from the border the cable started, the less East German curiosity would be aroused; however, a longer tunnel would also greatly increase the amount of dirt to be excavated and disposed of."

BODY-9   The tunnel lies in the southeast corner of the U.S. sector. While the warehouse in West Berlin was under construction, simultaneous operations were underway in Richmond, Virginia. Army engineers led by Lieutenant Colonel William R. Pogue of the Corps began building a test tunnel at the version was 450 feet long and had a depth of 30 feet, with a clearance of 3 feet between the roof and ground surface.

BODY-10   The East German border guards probably felt they harbored few illusions concerning the U.S. "warehouse." The building was surrounded by two barbed wire fences, powered by a diesel generator, equipped with a large parabolic antenna, and staffed by the U.S. Army Signal Corps. For all intents and purposes the area appeared to be a poorly concealed radar intercept station.

BODY-11   The overall CIA concept for the area called for observer confusion. In devising the engineering plans for the tunnel, the CIA devoted a great deal of thought to an appropriate "cover" for the project. A two-tiered solution was reached. The "warehouse" itself was deemed sufficiently innocuous to hide U.S. intentions during construction. To obfuscate activity during the tunnel's operational period the CIA decided to cover the site.

BODY-12   "REGAL became operational on 10 May 1955, and from the beginning collected a vast amount of information. According to Colonel Russell Horton, an Army Security Agency officer stationed in Berlin at the time, the collectors were 'turning out that stuff by the car loads.' Another analyst stated that they 'used to haul three or four mailbags back from Berlin' to Frankfurt at a time for initial processing."

BODY-13   Intercepted signals were relayed to the U.S. sector through the cables shown at the lower right corner of the passageway.

BODY-14   According to CIA officials interviewed after the termination of the operation, the biggest problem with the tunnel concerned the "quantity and content of the material available from the target and the manner in which it was to be processed." CIA officials kept strict control over who had access to tunnel information, using the same standards as those for Special Intelligence (SI). It was especially difficult to find adequately trained linguists cleared for SI to process the traffic. The CIA tested all its personnel with any knowledge of Russian or German for possible assignments as translators, but CIA resources were strained to the limit.

BODY-15   CIA and NSA fought over a great deal of the exchanged material. CIA was reluctant to give up its jurisdiction over the intelligence and refused to release certain information to NSA due to CIA rules and regulations concerning compartmentation of information. NSA, on the other hand, wanted to know everything concerning the CIA operation. Nielson recalled that when he would report back to NSA, General Burgess and I would debrief him on everything he saw at CIA to ensure that NSA received all REGAL reports.

BODY-22   "Between 17 and 22 April, all of the cables were inoperable at some point. On 22 April, the telephone lines for Marshal Andrei Antonovich Grechko, Commander, GFSG, and four of his generals, failed. A fault on cable FK150 eliminated all communications between Moscow and East Germany. Communications for the Soviet Air Warning Control Center also went down and Soviet Signal Troops and East German Post and Telegraph technicians were under enormous pressure to repair the damage."

BODY-24   "The monitors immediately halted operations and prepared for the backlash. The Soviet reaction was totally unexpected. C.S. intelligence experts assumed that the Soviet Union would not advertise the fact that its communications had been so totally compromised. However, the commandant of the Soviet Berlin Garrison, Major General Iosif Leontovich Zarenko, was away from Berlin at the time, and the Acting Commandant, Colonel Ivan A. Kotsyuba, decided to expose U.S. 'perfidy and treachery' to world opinion."

BODY-25   "It may have been during his three years of incarceration that Blake's political opinions were influenced to such an extent that he volunteered to work for the Soviets."

BODY-26   "Blake was sentenced to the maximum 42 years in prison because of his determination 'to wreak maximum vengeance' on Britain and its allies."

BODY-27   REGAL informed the U.S. and U~iet designs for Berlin and the "true story" behind officially reported activity.

BODY-28   The combined U.S.-U.K. effort, when viewed in terms of sheer volume, was a clear success. The monitored cables "contained metallic pairs capable of"

BODY-29   As a result - or, perhaps, as a weak justification for an expensive and not overwhelmingly successful undertaking- the CIA asserts that REGAL's most valuable legacy was not the intelligence derived, but the morale boost it gave the U.S. intelligence community at the expense of the Soviet Union and the sense of security inherent in the realization that Europe could not be the subject of a Soviet attack without U.S. foreknowledge.

BODY-30   NSA benefited immeasurably from its collaboration on the REGAL effort with the CIA and GCHQ because of the contacts made, the official exchanges, and the respect extended by the other collaborators for the NSA effort.

BODY-31   "The U.S. intelligence community obtained order of battle information during the tunnel construction through the close watch kept on the highway: analysts were able to ascertain the relative importance of visitors to East Berlin by the security measures implemented between the airport and the city."

BODY-32   "Between 1956 and 1958, CIA launched several hundred helium balloons equipped with observation cameras for travel over Eastern Europe and the Soviet Union. Although several balloons produced valuable information, many more fell or were *shot down over the Soviet Union, triggering official protests to Washington and alienating President Eisenhower."*

BODY-33   *"According to Sean Bourke, Blake boasted that 'the KGB knew about the tunnel before the first spadeful of earth was dug out of the ground. I saw to that.'" - Sean Bourke, The Springing of George Blake, p. 275.*

united states cryptologic history

Operation REGAL:

The Berlin Tunnel (S-CCO)

(b)(1)
(b)(3)-P.L. 86-36

UNITED STATES CRYPTOLOGIC HISTORY

Special Series

Number 4

Operation Regal:
The Berlin Tunnel (S-CCO)

(b)(3)-P.L. 86-36

NATIONAL SECURITY AGENCY/CENTRAL SECURITY SERVICE

1988

(b)(1)
(b)(3)-P.L. 86-36

DOCID: 3962741

Table of Contents

Foreword v

Prelude 1
Berlin: Challenge and Opportunity 2
Just the Right Spot 3
Masquerade 5
Digging In 6
.... 7
Completion . . . the Work Begins 7
Relying on a Rival 9
Intelligence Production 10
Some Interesting Sidelights 11
Strategy 12
Discovery 17
A Tunnel Opens to Mixed Reviews 17
Mole in the Tunnel? 20
Summing Up: Reassurance 21
And Misgivings 22
Crescendo and Decline 23
Legacy 24

Notes 26

(b)(1)

(b)(3)-P.L. 86-36

Foreword

(U) *Operation REGAL* is another volume in the United States Cryptologic History Special Report Series produced by the NSA History and Publications Division. REGAL was the codename for the Berlin Tunnel, a U.S. intelligence community operation conducted during the mid-1950s which was designed to intercept Soviet and East German communications.

(U) _____ began research on this subject in September 1985 while on an internship in the History and Publications Division. Working with NSA archival materials, oral interviews with key individuals, and CIA documents, _____ completed her study in late 1986. Concentrating on NSA involvement, she offers a number of interesting observations. She reveals that there was little cooperation initially between NSA and CIA regarding the Berlin Tunnel. Although the U.S. intelligence community at first considered REGAL a great success, the Soviets, thanks to George Blake, certainly knew about the operation early on, but apparently did not inform the East Germans of their discovery. Even the Soviet military may not have known (only the top officials of the KGB), leaving the tapped lines to be accidentally uncovered by the East Germans. It is an intriguing story, well told. And until the KGB opens its archives, precisely what the Soviets knew and when they knew it remain a mystery.

Henry F. Schorreck
NSA Historian

Operation REGAL

(TSC) *REGAL was the codename for the Berlin Tunnel, a U.S. intelligence community operation designed to intercept Soviet and East German communications. It involved the construction of an elaborate communications intercept center in a tunnel running beneath West Berlin into East Berlin. The tunnel was operational from 10 May 1955 until 21 April 1956 when the East Germans discovered the operation and closed it down. Despite its short operational period, REGAL was initially considered a great intelligence success by U.S. officials because of the large volume of information intercepted. There was also an initial feeling of accomplishment in carrying out such an elaborate intelligence scheme literally underneath the feet of the Soviet and East German military. Later developments led U.S. intelligence community analysts, however, to question the validity of the intercepted information and its importance relative to the expense undertaken in constructing the tunnel. Considered a major Central Intelligence Agency (CIA) operation by the American press, the National Security Agency (NSA) nevertheless played a vital role in the project. This is a study of NSA's involvement in REGAL.*

Prelude

(b)(1)
(b)(3)
OGA

CIA

(S) Due to the increased use of ultra-high frequency line-of-sight radio communications after World War II, _____ leaving British and American officials desperate for information on Soviet intentions. Before the introduction of high frequency, shortwave communications, airwaves could be monitored at great distances from the actual source because long, low frequency waves bend around the earth. However, the transmitting of large volumes of communications beyond high frequency presented a problem for the British and American analysts as these waves are basically line-of-sight. Alternate intercept methods therefore had to be devised to fill the collection void.[3]

(b)(1)
(b)(3)-50 USC 4
(b)(3)-P.L. 86-36

(U) _____ CIA's Office of Communications accidentally opened the way to new intercept possibilities when he discovered a way to exploit landline messages. SIGTOT, a Bell System Cipher machine used by the United States in global communications, had been rejected by the U.S. government for secure communications during World War II because of its vulnerability to intercept. To their chagrin, Bell technicians discovered that as SIGTOT electrically encrypted a message, faint "echoes"[4] of the plain text were transmitted along the wire simultaneously with the enciphered message. Refusing to accept Bell's modifications to its 131-B2 mixer, the Army Signal

(b)(1)
(b)(3)-P.L. 86-36

Corps abandoned SIGTOT as a vehicle for wartime encryption, and the machine's peculiarity faded into oblivion until rediscovered _____ in 1951.[5]

(U) _____ suspected that SIGTOT's vulnerability, which enabled him to tap into a cable carrying the enciphered message and read the plain text without deciphering probably existed in other systems. He set out to prove his hypothesis.

_____ Despite being a close ally, however, the British were not informed of _____ discovery.[7]

(TSC) Keenly interested in the intercept possibilities, the CIA hoped to use _____ innovation to exploit Soviet landlines in East Berlin. _____ findings coincided with the discovery by

_____ Rowlett had joined the CIA as a Special Assistant to the Director of Central Intelligence.[8] After five years with CIA, Rowlett returned to NSA in 1958.

(b)(1)
(b)(3)-P.L. 86-36

Berlin: Challenge and Opportunity

(U) Because of the nature of the pre-World War II communications system, Berlin was the central circuit of East European communications. Any calls originating in Eastern Europe were channeled through Berlin, including all calls to Moscow. Monitoring Berlin's communications would greatly increase the U.S. Soviet-Eastern Europe collection effort. Berlin's telephone and telegraph system resembled a wheel, with two concentric circles spanning East and West Berlin. Switching stations, placed at strategic locations around the circle, directed service to each city sector via lines like the spokes of a wheel. The occupying officials divided the city after the war and disconnected the telephone lines from the terminals. To tap into the East Berlin system the CIA needed to reconnect the lines and monitor the cables.[9]

(S) William King Harvey, CIA Bureau Chief in Berlin, enthusiastically pursued the idea of exploiting Berlin communications. Under Harvey's direction the CIA attempted various tapping methods and by January 1953 had obtained a 15-minute sample of a "prime target circuit."[10]

(b)(1)
(b)(3)
OGA

CIA

(U) The CIA realized that Berlin inherently posed more difficulties for the tunnel-builders than had Vienna. The border area was under constant scrutiny from East German guards. Without arousing undue suspicion, construction workers would have to burrow from West Berlin under the heavily guarded border into East Berlin in order to tap the cables.

(S) Never having undertaken such a project, the CIA enlisted British aid in its development, recognizing British expertise in the "highly specialized art of vertical tunneling."[13] The trick entailed digging through soft soil without collapsing the roof. Harvey negotiated with the British and devised the following divisions of responsibility. The CIA was to "(1) procure a site, erect the necessary structures, and drive a tunnel to a point beneath the target cables; (2) be responsible for the recording of all signals produced at the point where the 'lead-away' tapping cables entered the installation; and (3) process in Washington all of the telegraphic materials received from the project."

(b) (1)
(b) (3)
OGA

CIA

Just the Right Spot

(S) Before Harvey laid out his final plans for Washington's approval, an appropriate site had to be selected. The tunnel had to originate in either the U.S. or U.K. zones in Berlin, with a path in range of the targeted cables. The farther from the border the cable started, the less East German curiosity would be aroused; however, a longer tunnel would also greatly increase the amount of dirt to be excavated and disposed of. Both the operators and the equipment required fresh air, which also set a limit on the length of the tunnel because of the maximum capabilities of the air pumps. The small CIA REGAL planning team finally decided on a spot originating in the U.S. zone where land could be purchased to build the above-ground compound and from which the tunnel length was feasible. Collateral information on the site was also available, identifying the target cable plan, aerial photographs, and utility lines. Geological maps indicated that the area was predominantly flat, with soft soil but uneven drainage. The permanent water table was deemed to be 32 feet below ground. Because of the importance of isolating the electronic equipment from damp areas, the supposedly low water table would aid the engineers by eliminating requirements for watertight construction.[15]

(S) Armed with technical data, William Harvey returned to Washington to obtain official approval for REGAL. He briefed CIA Director Allen Dulles, Clandestine Services Chief Frank Wisner, and Deputy Clandestine Services Chief Richard Helms concerning his meetings with the British and the blueprints for the tunnel's construction and operations. Dulles approved Harvey's plans, directing, however, that "in the interest of security as little as possible should be reduced to writing."[16] The U.S. side followed Dulles's stipulation scrupulously, but the British retained extensive notes of the proceedings. Minutes of the initial meeting between Harvey and the British were kept by an MI-6 agent, George Blake.[17] However, CIA officials decided not to inform the rest of the intelligence community of the project, not even NSA.

(S) The tunnel operation got underway in 1954 with the construction of a two-story warehouse in West Berlin over the area chosen to be one terminus of the tunnel. Although the construction workers would not comprehend the purpose of a two-story warehouse with a basement requiring a 12-foot ceiling, its large size was required to hold the expected 3,000 tons of dirt excavated from 1,476 foot long, $6\frac{1}{2}$ foot wide tunnel. The main floor housed the electronic equipment.[18]

Berlin, the Divided City.
The tunnel lies in the southeast corner of the U.S. sector.

(b)(1)
(b)(3)
OGA

CIA

(S) While the warehouse in West Berlin was under construction, simultaneous operations were underway in ▮▮▮▮▮▮▮ and Richmond, Virginia. Army engineers led by Lieutenant Colonel Leslie M. Gross of the Engineering Crops began building a test tunnel at the ▮▮▮▮▮▮▮▮▮▮▮▮[19] The ▮▮▮▮▮▮▮ version was 450 feet long and dug at a depth of 20 feet, with 13½ feet between the roof and ground surface. Meanwhile, equipment for the Berlin job was assembled in Richmond. Among the supplies were 125 tons of steel liner plates which when joined created the tunnel's walls. The plates were specially treated with a protective rubber coat to suppress noise during construction. The gathered supplies then went by ship to ▮▮▮▮▮▮▮▮▮▮▮ and by train to Berlin and the completed warehouse near Altglienecke.[20]

The site in enlargement, detailing the West Berlin suburban area from which the tunnel began.

Masquerade

(U) The East German border guards probably felt they harbored few illusions concerning the U.S. "warehouse." The building was surrounded by two barbed wire fences, powered by a diesel generator, equipped with a large parabolic antenna, and staffed by the U.S. Army Signal Corps. For all intents and purposes the area appeared to be a poorly concealed radar intercept station.

(b) (1)
(b) (3)-50 USC 403
(b) (3)-P.L. 86-36

SECRET

(S) The overall CIA concept for the area called for observer confusion. In devising the engineering plans for the tunnel, the CIA devoted a great deal of thought to an appropriate "cover" for the project. A two-tiered solution was reached. The "warehouse" itself was deemed sufficiently innocuous to hide U.S. intentions during construction. To obfuscate activity during the tunnel's operational period, the CIA decided to cover the site

b)(1)
b)(3)
OGA

(U) Americans and Germans in the western sector were also curious about the area, and their interest was fed by a series of unusual incidents. A civilian engineer originally heading the construction project quit after publicly protesting the need for such an immense basement. Civilians actually constructing the building were required to wear Army Signal Corps uniforms without explanation.[22] Speculation was abundant, but little of substance was learned as the few actually cognizant of the intricacies of the operation were not talking.

(S) By 17 August 1954, the German contractors had completed their work, and the U.S. had possession of the compound. All supplies, shipped under disguise and strict security, were in Berlin awaiting the start of construction. Simultaneously, a tunnel group at the CIA's Office of Communications designed the "unique equipment" required to process the expected telegraphic material. A great deal of care went into the selection of components for the taps and electrical equipment. All pieces were scrupulously tested for reliability and constructed of the best materials.[23]

Digging In

(U) Construction of the tunnel was a laborious, time-consuming task, complicated by surveillance and security risks. Beginning in the basement's easternmost point, the engineers

> sank a vertical shaft 18 feet in diameter to a depth of 20 feet, then drove pilings halfway into the floor of the shaft. Next, a steel ring $6\frac{1}{2}$ feet in diameter and fitted with hydraulic jacks around its circumference was lowered into place. Braced against the exposed section of the pilings, the ring, or "shield," was fitted flush against the tunnel's face.[24]

(S) Three-man shifts using picks and shovels worked on the tunnel's construction 24 hours a day. Gains were small: the team excavated two inches, shoved the shield forward, and then repeated the process. After they had excavated an entire foot, the engineers bolted a steel liner plate onto already bolted plates to form the tunnel wall. They lined the tunnel with steel so that the walls would not implode due to the large percentage of sand in the soil.[25] The plates each contained small holes which the engineers unplugged and filled with cement to pack any space left between the dirt and the wall. After six feet had been completed, the existing wall was secure enough to brace the jacked-forward shield, and the engineers removed the hydraulic jacks from the process.[26]

(S) The tedious process was slowed because of the security demands placed upon the engineers. A lookout kept watch around the clock to observe any signs of undue suspicion or curiosity on the part of the East Germans. Whenever German guards walked over the work area, the team halted construction. Building plans called for as quiet an operation as steel and hydraulic jacks could allow. The U.S. team finished the tunnel shell on 28

DOCID: 3962741

TOP SECRET UMBRA

(b)(1)

February 1955, complete with a steel and concrete "anti-personnel" door on the East Berlin side to prevent East German officials from storming the tunnel upon discovery.[27]

CIA

Completion... the Work Begins

(S) The finished tunnel was 1,486 feet long, with the first half sloping downward and the second half sloping upward. To keep the equipment and the cables dry, the Army engineers installed pumps on both sides and panelled the section adjoining the tap chamber with "marine-type plywood" for insulation.[35]

(S) While the engineers completed the tunnel, CIA personnel fabricated a contingency plan to be effected upon discovery of the tunnel by the East Germans. The U.S. would publicly deny all knowledge of the tunnel. Secretly, the operatives were to defend against forced entry, activate the anti-personnel door, and if necessary, demolish the tunnel with charges mined at the border.[36]

(TSC) REGAL became operational on 10 May 1955, and from the beginning collected a vast amount of information. According to Colonel Russell Horton, an Army Security Agency officer stationed in Berlin at the time, the collectors were "turning out that stuff by the car loads."[37] Another analyst stated that they "used to haul three or four mailbags back from Berlin" to Frankfurt at a time for initial processing.[38] U.S. personnel monitored the tunnel inside and out 24 hours a day.

(b)(1)
(b)(3)-50 USC 403
(b)(3)-18 USC 798
(b)(3)-P.L. 86-36

7

TOP SECRET UMBRA

A Soviet photograph taken from just beyond the chamber where the landline taps were applied. Intercepted signals were relayed to the U.S. sector through the cables shown at the lower right corner of the passageway.

8

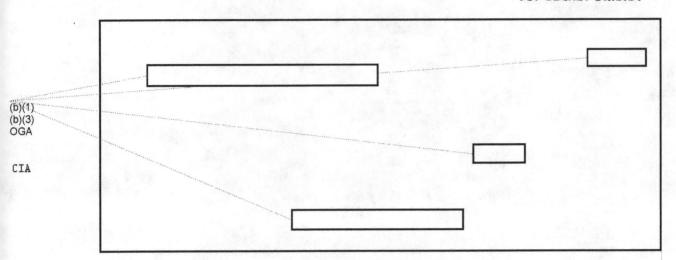

(b)(1)
(b)(3)
OGA

CIA

Relying on a Rival

(S) According to CIA officials interviewed after the termination of the operation, the biggest problem with the tunnel concerned the "quantity and content of the material available from the target and the manner in which it was to be processed."[44] CIA officials kept strict control over who had access to tunnel information, using the same standards as those for Special Intelligence (SI).[45] It was especially difficult to find adequately trained linguists cleared for SI to process the traffic. The CIA tested all its personnel with any knowledge of Russian or German for possible assignments as translators,[46] but CIA resources were strained to the limit. Only then was material given to NSA linguists.

(b)(1)
(b)(3)-50 USC 403
(b)(3)-18 USC 798
(b)(3)-P.L. 86-36

DOCID: 3962741

TOP SECRET UMBRA

(b)(3)-P.L. 86-36

(TS-CCO) CIA and NSA fought over a great deal of the exchanged material. CIA was reluctant to give up its jurisdiction over the intelligence and refused to release certain information to NSA due to CIA rules and regulations concerning compartmentation of information. NSA, on the other hand, wanted to know everything concerning the CIA operation. Nielson recalled that when he would report back to NSA, General Burgess and [_____] would debrief him on everything he saw at CIA to ensure that NSA received all REGAL reports. Two former NSA analysts, [_____] headed the CIA L Building operation, and these two "smooth numbers" were often "slow to give" up REGAL intelligence. [_____]

[50] It was a touchy situation.

Intelligence Production

(E)(1)
(b)(3)-50 USC 403
(b)(3)-18 USC 798
(b)(3)-P.L. 86-36

(TSC) On 6 June 1955 the Washington REGAL Center (WRC) issued the first intelligence report based on the [   ] The WRC aperiodic reports were classified "TOP SECRET REGAL" and occasionally contained the codeword "EIDER." The Main Processing Unit in London issued aperiodic intelligence reports under the title JMTRS, which expanded to Joint Military Translation and Reporting Service.

(TSC) The intelligence reports issued by the WRC and the JMTRS usually contained several unrelated items in a format similar to a weekly activity summary. Previously reported items were often referenced as new information became available. Major topics

(b)(1)
(b)(3)
OGA

CIA

Some Interesting Sidelights

Strategy

TOP SECRET UMBRA

(b)(1)
(b)(3)-18 USC 798
(b)(3)-50 USC 403
(b)(3)-P.L. 86-36

(b)(1)
(b)(3)
OGA

CIA

(b)(1)
(b)(3)-P.L. 86-36

DOCID: 3962741

(b)(1)
(b)(3)-18 USC 798
(b)(3)-50 USC 403
(b)(3)-P.L. 86-36

(b)(1)
(b)(3)
OGA

CIA

(TS-CCO) As stated earlier, most of NSA's involvement in the tunnel operation occurred after the tunnel was discovered. Only James Nielson and a handful of other high-level NSA analysts were aware of the existence of the covert CIA operation until it was exposed. Although the CIA realized that the tunnel would be discovered eventually and the collection operation shutdown, no one could have foreseen the circumstances that led to its disclosure.

Discovery

(TS-CCO) On 21 April 1956, eleven months and eleven days after the U.S. first began monitoring Soviet and East German communications, an East German repair crew uncovered the tapped cables. Dr. Nielson recalled going to work one morning and being told "It's all over."[99] Several days of heavy rainfall had flooded the low-lying areas, and while the pumps on the U.S. side of the tunnel were powerful enough to keep the electrical equipment dry, the pumps on the East German side were not strong enough to do so, resulting in an electrical short.[100] Between 17 and 22 April, all of the cables were inoperable at some point.[101]

(S) On 22 April, the telephone lines for Marshal Andrei Antonovich Grechko, Commander, GFSG, and four of his generals, failed. A fault on cable FK150 eliminated all communications between Moscow and East Germany. Communications for the Soviet Air Warning Control Center also went down and Soviet Signal Troops and East German Post and Telegraph technicians were under enormous pressure to repair the damage. While digging to reach the cable on 22 April, the technicians uncovered the tap chamber at about 0200 hours. The tap chamber microphone at that time picked up the conversation and activity going on around it. Unaware of the significance of their discovery, the technicians continued to dig, finally leaving the site at 0330 to report their findings. It was not until 0630 that the microphone picked up the announcement that "the cable is tapped." Soon afterwards, the East German telephone operators refused to place any outgoing telephone calls, saying that it was against "orders."[102] The intercept operators realized that the end was imminent.

A Tunnel Opens to Mixed Reviews

(S) The entire chamber was uncovered and entered around 1300, when pictures and measurements were taken. The East Germans expressed "wonder and admiration" at the technology and ingenuity involved. The last interesting phone calls were placed in the 0800 hour, and the teletype traffic stopped at 1530 when the tap wires were cut. The

A close-up view of the tunnel's receiver bays and watertight casing.
The sandbags along the sides provided sound proofing and insulation.

microphone was dismantled at 1550, and REGAL could no longer intercept intelligence.[103] The monitors immediately halted operations and prepared for the backlash.

(TS) The Soviet reaction was totally unexpected. U.S. intelligence experts assumed that the Soviet Union would not advertise the fact that its communications had been so totally compromised.[104] However, the commandant of the Soviet Berlin Garrison, Major General Iosif Leontovich Zarenko, was away from Berlin at the time, and the Acting Commandant, Colonel Ivan A. Kotsyuba, decided to expose U.S. "perfidy and treachery" to world opinion. On 23 April Kotsyuba called a press conference to elucidate on U.S. spy activity. Expressing "righteous indignation,"[105] the Soviets apparently hoped to exploit the situation to their advantage and curtail Allied activities to Berlin.[106] With the U.S. "warehouse" looming as the obvious endpoint of the tunnel, the Soviets accused the U.S. of tapping "important underground long-distance telephone" lines linking Berlin with other nations.[107] They conducted official tours of the tunnel and allowed Western press members to cross underground into West Berlin. Exploitation of this "illegal and intolerable action"[108] led to carnival-like enterprise on the East Berlin side, complete with snack bar, as about 90,000 East Berlin citizens toured "the capitalist warmongers' expensive subterranean listening post."[109]

(C) The U.S. and West German reactions to the accusation and notoriety were subdued and guarded. The U.S. Army denied knowledge of the tunnel but promised to undertake an immediate investigation.[110] Little doubt existed among the press that it was a joint U.S.-British operation – the electrical equipment found in the tunnel was stamped "Made in England," while the tunnel pumps were determined to be of U.S. manufacture.[111] However, the operation amused and delighted the general public in the West. Even Soviet technicians expressed admiration for a tap chamber that resembled the "communications center of a battleship,"[112] and American journalists considered ingenious its construction literally underneath the feet of the Soviet and East German militaries.[113] The Western press considered it quite an intelligence coup.

(U) The Soviet propaganda effort, undertaken in satellite countries as well as the West following the tunnel's discovery,[114] appeared to backfire, giving the U.S. and the CIA very favorable publicity. Even the later East German claim that the tunnel idea had been originated by Eleanor Dulles, sister of the Secretary of State and at the time Special Assistant to the Director of the Department of State's Office of German Affairs,[115] failed to elicit sympathy. The press and the general public assumed that Soviet and East German communications had been compromised for almost a year without detection.

(S-CCO) Although the uncovering of the tunnel had come about sooner than expected by Western intelligence officials, they considered the East German discovery "purely fortuitous"[116] and the unpredictable result of poor weather and bad luck. The failed cable had been known to be in poor condition, and the British had therefore delayed activating the tap until 2 August 1955, more than two months later than the other two taps.[117] However, conflicting opinions soon began to emerge as to the reasons behind the premature demise ▮▮▮▮▮▮ Privately some U.S. officials believed that only a senior official could have betrayed the REGAL operation at such an early time. Frank Rowlett felt that the Soviets "very clumsily put on an act of discovery."[118] However, no hard evidence was obtained until the 1961 revelation of the Soviet spy activities of MI-6 agent George Blake, the very official who had taken such careful notes in the British-American discussions concerning the tunnel.

(b) (1)
(b) (3)
OGA

CIA

(b)(1)
(b)(3)-P.L. 86-36
(b)(3)-50 USC 403

George Blake, a Soviet double agent within British Intelligence (MI-6), had intimate knowledge of Operation REGAL.

Mole in the Tunnel?

(U) Born the son of an Egyptian Jew in Rotterdam, George Blake escaped from the Netherlands to Spain on a forged passport during World War II. From Spain he went to Britain where he joined the British Navy and served heroically with Naval Intelligence during the war. Initially recruited by the British Secret Service in 1944, Blake studied Russian at Cambridge in 1947 and was appointed a Vice-Consul with the British Foreign Service the following year. Assigned to Seoul in 1948, Blake, along with the other British Embassy officials, was captured by North Korean Communists in 1950. It may have been during his three years of incarceration that Blake's political opinions were influenced to such an extent that he volunteered to work for the Soviets. Released in April 1953, Blake rejoined British intelligence as an MI-6 secret agent in 1954.[119] The fact that his cousin Henri Curiel was one of the founding members of the Egyptian Communist Party was apparently not taken into account in his appointment. When arrested in 1961 after being unmasked by a Polish defector, Blake pled guilty to the espionage charges, saying that since 1953 he had given every important document with which he came in contact to his Soviet contact.[120] Charged with "communicating information that might be directly or indirectly useful to an enemy power"[121] and three violations of the Official Secrets Act,[122] Blake was sentenced to the maximum 42 years in prison because of his determination "to wreak maximum vengeance" on Britain and its allies.[123]

(TS-CCO) Officially, the U.S. reacted rather calmly to the news of Blake's spy activities. The Department of State held a press conference to state that Blake had apparently not compromised any U.S. secrets.[124] Unofficially, however, there was a great deal of consternation among the officials involved with the tunnel operation. Frank Rowlett remembered Blake's presence at a U.S.-British meeting on tunnel details in Britain in 1951 and believed that Blake "was well aware of what we were doing" and must have passed the information on to the Soviets.[125] [redacted] CIA's Office of Communications said that Blake "knew every detail" of the tunnel operation.[126] In retrospect, the CIA realized that Blake had apparently also previously compromised the

[redacted]

American intelligence now had to speculate that perhaps the Soviets had allowed REGAL to operate for almost a year[128] in order to protect their valuable source in British intelligence.[129]

(b)(1)
(b)(3)
OGA

CIA

[redacted]

Summing Up: Reassurance...

[redacted]

(b)(1)
(b)(3)-50 USC 403
(b)(3)-18 USC 798
(b)(3)-P.L. 86-36

(b)(1)
(b)(3)-50 USC 403
(b)(3)-18 USC 798
(b)(3)-P.L. 86-36

TOP SECRET UMBRA

(S) While NSA concentrated on specific, technical information gained from intercept, REGAL satisfied other objectives for the CIA. The CIA called REGAL a "unique source of current intelligence of a kind and quality which had not been available since 1948," and the primary source on Soviet intentions in Europe.[136] In the political sphere, REGAL informed the U.S. and U.K. of Soviet designs for Berlin and the "true story" behind officially reported activity. [   ] intercept also established that the Soviets were determined to maintain their sphere of influence vis-a-vis the other occupying powers in Berlin, despite East German attempts at sovereignty.[137]

(S) REGAL intercept allowed the United States to notify its representatives at the 1955 Foreign Ministers Conference in Geneva that the Soviets had decided to establish an East German Army, and the REGAL account of the attempted implementation of the Soviet 20th Party Congress decisions indicated that dissent among Soviet nuclear scientists, aroused by the denunciation of Stalin and the era of collective leadership, was being suppressed. The intercept also followed Marshal Georgiy Konstantonovich Zhukov's downfall as he attempted to decrease the power of Soviet Armed Forces political officers.[138]

P.L. 86-36
50 USC 403

... And Misgivings

(TSC) After George Blake's conviction, the question of the validity of REGAL intelligence was combined with doubts concerning its intelligence value. American intelligence officials could not ignore the possibility of a massive disinformation campaign mounted by the Soviets. Although they determined that it was highly unlikely that the Soviets and East Germans had the time, funds, and inclination to undertake such an immense effort,[140] speculation continued on possible precautionary measures the Soviets may have taken. Because the evidence presented at Blake's trial was never made public, it is not known when (and/or whether) he actually informed the Soviets about the tunnel. To protect himself, Blake may have delayed presenting the information, realizing that he might be suspected if the Soviets "discovered" the tunnel immediately upon its becoming operational. On the other hand, the Soviets themselves may have deliberately postponed exposing REGAL in order to protect Blake.

(TS-CCO) The cause of REGAL's exposure has not been, and probably never will be, ascertained. Frank Rowlett believed that the Soviets deliberately exposed the tunnel on 21 April 1956 for their own unknown reasons. At the time, the CIA determined that it was the unpredictable result of bad luck. Perhaps only a few Soviet officials and George Blake ever knew for sure. However, the presence of bad weather, flooded cables, and electrical shorts are indisputable facts. Despite Soviet knowledge of the intercept operation and unanswered questions concerning the validity of the information, it is very probable that REGAL's exposure was the unexpected result of poor weather rather than any deliberate Soviet initiative. To understand possible Soviet motives concerning the tunnel, the two types of monitored communications – telephone and teleprinter wires – must be examined separately.

(S) Based on the confused GSFG reaction to the tunnel discovery, the CIA concluded that the East Germans happened upon REGAL by chance. Subsequent revelations about Blake did not provide sufficient evidence to refute this determination. If Blake did disclose REGAL, it seems he'd have no problem providing sufficient information for the Soviets to find the approximate location.

Crescendo and Decline

(S) The combined U.S.-U.K. effort, when viewed in terms of sheer volume, was a clear success. The ___ monitored cables "contained ___ metallic pairs capable of

DOCID: 3962741

(b)(1)
(b)(3)
OGA

CIA

TOP SECRET UMBRA

transmitting a total of approximately ▢ communication channels," with up to ▢ in use at any one time.[141] On the average, the monitors recorded ▢ telegraphic circuits and ▢ voice circuits continuously, resulting in about ▢ reels of magnetic tape totaling about ▢ tons.[142]

(S) The personnel who processed REGAL material were spread out among several organizations. MPU in London employed ▢ persons who transcribed ▢ Soviet two-hour voice reels containing ▢ conversations. MPU processed ▢ of the ▢ German voice reels received, fully transcribing ▢ conversations.[143] Many of the transcribers remained with the organization after it became the London Processing Group (LPG), working under James Nielson when he served as the first U.S. LPG Deputy Branch Chief.[144]

(S) In Washington, ▢ people at TPU processed ▢ six-hour Soviet teletype reels and ▢ six-hour German teletype reels. Some of the reels had as many as ▢ separate circuits which used time-division multiplexing to create additional circuits. The CIA stationed a small crew of two to four persons in Berlin for immediate monitoring of crucial intelligence and maintaining security.[145] The number of NSA employees included in the TPU figures has been impossible to ascertain as NSA was not mentioned in the official CIA history of REGAL. The exact number of NSA analysts, supervisors, and clerical workers processing REGAL material is also unknown because the numbers changed monthly due to varying requirements and part-time personnel. GENS-14 kept thorough records of NSA REGAL personnel in the beginning of the operation, but less inclusive documentation as time progressed. As of December 1956 REGAL processing employed about ▢ NSA personnel either at AHS or Fort Meade.[146]

Legacy

(TSC) Operation REGAL involved various intelligence community members – CIA, NSA, Army, and GCHQ – between its planning stage in the early 1950s and the end of REGAL intercept processing in 1958. Vast amounts of information of varying degrees of intelligence interest were intercepted. Numerous engineers, monitors, processors, analysts, managers, and linguists aided the ostentatious and expensive effort. In retrospect, ▢

▢ As a result – or, perhaps, as a weak justification for an expensive and not overwhelmingly successful undertaking – the CIA asserts that REGAL's most valuable legacy was not the intelligence derived, but the morale boost it gave the U.S. intelligence community at the expense of the Soviet Union and the sense of security inherent in the realization that Europe could not be the subject of a Soviet attack without U.S. foreknowledge.

(TS-CCO) NSA's motives for its REGAL participation distinguished it from CIA, and its goals and expectations were correspondingly distinct. NSA did not receive accolades for its part in the operation for several reasons. It was the CIA which ingeniously engineered and constructed the tunnel and equipment, while NSA officially included only about a dozen individuals in the actual covert intercept operation. NSA conducted its endeavors predominantly in the 18 months following the intercept shutdown, by which time the tunnel's color and appeal had waned. CIA operatives deserved credit for their glamorous operation, despite REGAL's probable exposure by Blake. NSA did not want public recognition, but wanted instead what the agency believed was more valuable – its acceptance by U.S. intelligence community members as a viable and equal contributor to the intelligence effort. There was a great deal of competition between the CIA and NSA at the time, and NSA, as the less established of the two, felt compelled to prove its worth. REGAL provided an opportunity CIA, unable to process REGAL material adequately, reluctantly recruited NSA assistance, thereby formally recognizing NSA analytic skills. Consequently, in addition to the intelligence it obtained from ⬜⬜⬜⬜ NSA benefited immeasurably from its collaboration on the REGAL effort with the CIA and GCHQ because of the contacts made, the official exchanges, and the respect extended by the other collaborators for the NSA effort.

(b)(1)
(b)(3)
OGA

CIA

(b)(1)
(b)(3)-50 USC 403
(b)(3)-P.L. 86-36

NOTES

1. (U) [   ] Frank Rowlett. "The Berlin Tunnel Operation: 1952–1956," 24 June 1969, Clandestine Services History, No. 150, CIA. (S)
2. (U) David C. Martin, *Wilderness of Mirrors* (New York: Harper and Row, Publishers, 1980), p. 73. (U)
3. (U) [   ] Rowlett, "Tunnel." (S)
4. (U) Martin, *Wilderness*, p. 74. (U)
5. (U) Martin, *Wilderness*, p. 74. (U)
6. (U) Martin, *Wilderness*, p. 74. (U)
7. (U) Martin, *Wilderness*, p. 74. (U)
8. (U) Interview Philip Dibben, 10 May 1985 by Robert D. Farley, OH 09-85, NSA. (TSC SENS/LIMDIS)
9. (U) Martin, *Wilderness*, p. 75. (U)
10. (U) [   ] Rowlett, "Tunnel." (S)
11. (U) [   ] Rowlett, "Tunnel." (S)
12. (U) Martin, *Wilderness*, p. 76. (U)
13. (U) Martin, *Wilderness*, p. 76. (U)
14. (U) [   ] Rowlett, "Tunnel." (S)
15. (U) [   ] Rowlett, "Tunnel." (S)
16. (U) Martin, *Wilderness*, p. 78. (U)
17. (U) E. H. Cookridge, *The Many Sides of George Blake Esq.: The Complete Dossier* (Princeton: Brandon/Systems Press, Inc., 1970) p. 158; Martin, p. 100. (U)
18. (U) [   ] Rowlett, "Tunnel." (S)
19. (U) [   ] Rowlett, "Tunnel." (S)
20. (U) Martin, *Wilderness*, p. 79. (U)
21. (U) [   ] Rowlett, "Tunnel." (S)
22. (U) "Wonderful Tunnel," *Time*, (7 May 1956) 67:42. (U)
23. (U) [   ] Rowlett, "Tunnel." (S)
24. (U) Martin, *Wilderness*, p. 80. (U)
25. (U) [   ] Rowlett, "Tunnel." (S)
26. (U) Martin, *Wilderness*, p. 80. (U)
27. (U) [   ] Rowlett, "Tunnel." (S)
28. (U) [   ] Rowlett, "Tunnel." (S)
29. (U) Martin, *Wilderness*, p. 82. (U)
30. (U) The U.S. intelligence community obtained order of battle information during the tunnel construction through the close watch kept on the highway: analysts were able to ascertain the relative importance of visitors to East Berlin by the security measures implemented between the airport and the city.
31. (U) [   ] Rowlett, "Tunnel."(S)
32. (U) Martin, *Wilderness*, p. 83. (U)
33. (U) Martin, *Wilderness*, p. 83. (U)
34. (U) [   ] Rowlett, "Tunnel." (S)
35. (U) [   ] Rowlett, "Tunnel." (S)
36. (U) [   ] Rowlett, "Tunnel." (S)
37. (U) Interview Colonel Russel Horton, 24 March 1982, 8 April 1982, 23 April 1982 by Robert D. Farley, OH 06-82, NSA. (TSC)
38. (U) Dibben interview, OH 09-85. (TSC SENS/LIMDIS)
39. (U) Interview Dr. James R. Nielson, 21 July 1986 by Robert D. Farley [   ] OH 20-86, NSA. (TS-CCO)
40. (U) Horton interview, OH 06-82. (TSC)
41. (U) [   ] Intercept: Landline Cables in East Berlin," 1 April 1957, Series VI, I.3.5, Historical Collection, NSA. Hereinafter cited as "[   ] Intercept." (TSC)
42. (U) Martin, *Wilderness*, p. 84. (U)

44. (U) [   ] Rowlett, "Tunnel." (S)
45. (U) Special intelligence refers to a category of sensitive compartmented information requiring special controls for restricted handling within compartmented intelligence systems and for which compartmentation is established. Compartmentation is a formal system of restricted access to intelligence activities, such systems established by and/or managed under the cognizance of the Director of Central Intelligence to protect the sensitive aspect of sources, methods, and analytical procedures of foreign intelligence programs.
46. (U) [   ] Rowlett, "Tunnel." (S)
47. (U) Nielson interview, OH 20-86. (TS-CCO)

(b)(1)
(b)(3)-18 USC 798
(b)(3)-50 USC 403
(b)(3)-P.L. 86-36

(b)(1)
(b)(3)
OGA

CIA

(b)(3)-P.L. 86-36

(b)(1)
(b)(3)-50 USC 403
(b)(3)-P.L. 86-36

48. (U) Nielson interview, OH 20-86. (TS-CCO)
49. (U) Nielson interview, OH 20-86. (TS-CCO)
50. (U) Nielson interview, OH 20-86. (TS-CCO)
51. (U) Nielson interview, OH 20-86. (TS-CCO)
52. (U) Martin. *Wilderness*, p. 84. (U)
53. (U) ▮▮▮▮▮ Intercept." (TSC)
54. (U) Interview Jane E. Dunn, 29 June 1981 by Robert D. Farley, OH 05-81, NSA. (TSC)
55. (U) GENS was one of four major operational divisions of NSA's Production Organization; it combined later with ADVA (Advanced Soviet) into A Group.
56. (U) Nielson interview, OH 20-86. (TS-CCO)
57. (U) Nielson interview, OH 20-86. (TS-CCO)
58. (U) Interview Dr. James R. Nielson, 14 May 1980 by Robert D. Farley and Henry Schorreck, OH 18-80, NSA. (S-CCO)
59. (U) Dunn interview, OH 05-81. (TSC)
60. (U) ▮▮▮▮▮ Intercept." (TSC)
61. (S) Between 1956 and 1958, CIA launched several hundred helium balloons equipped with observation cameras for travel over Eastern Europe and the Soviet Union. Although several balloons produced valuable information, many more fell or were shot down over the Soviet Union, triggering official protests to Washington and alienating President Eisenhower. See Donald E. Welzenbach, "Observation Balloons and Reconnaissance Satellites," *Studies in Intelligence* (Spring 1986) 30:21-28. (S)
62. (U) Washington REGAL Center Intelligence Report, 28 May 1956, Cryptologic Archival Holding Area, NSA. (TSC)
63. (U) Nielson interview, OH 20-86. (TSC)
64. (U) ▮▮▮▮▮ Intercept." (TSC)
65. (U) ▮▮▮▮▮ Intercept." (TSC)
66. (U) Dibben interview, OH 09-85. (TSC SENS/LIMDIS)
67. (U) Nielson interview, OH 20-86. (TS-CCO)
68. (U) GENS-143 Monthly Operation Summary, July 1956, Accession Number 10243, Cryptologic Archival Holding Area, NSA. (TS EIDER ▮▮▮▮▮
69. (U) GENS-143 Monthly Operation Summary, August 1956, Accession Number 10243, Cryptologic Archival Holding Area, NSA. (TS EIDER ▮▮▮▮▮
70. (U) GENS-143 Monthly Operation Summary, July 1956, Accession Number 10243, Cryptologic Archival Holding Area, NSA. (TS EIDER ▮▮▮▮▮
71. (U) GENS-143 Monthly Operation Summary, December 1956, Accession Number 10243, Cryptologic Archival Holding Area, NSA. (TS EIDER ▮▮▮▮▮
72. (U) GENS-143 Monthly Operation Summary, August 1956, Accession Number 10243, Cryptologic Archival Holding Area, NSA. (TS EIDER ▮▮▮▮▮
73. (U) GENS-14 Monthly Operation Summary, October 1956, Accession Number 10243, Cryptologic Archival Holding Area, NSA. (TS EIDER ▮▮▮▮▮
74. (U) GENS-14 Monthly Operation Summary, October 1956, Accession Number 10243, Cryptologic Holding Archival Area, NSA. (TS EIDER ▮▮▮▮▮
75. (U) GENS-143 Monthly Operation Summary, August 1956, Accession Number 10243, Cryptologic Archival Holding Area, NSA. (TS EIDER ▮▮▮▮▮
76. (U) GENS-14 Monthly Operation Summary, December 1956, Accession Number 10243, Cryptologic Archival Holding Area, NSA. (TS EIDER ▮▮▮▮▮
77. (U) GENS-143 Monthly Operation Summary, September 1956, Accession Number 10243, Cryptologic Archival Holding Area, NSA. (TS EIDER ▮▮▮▮▮
78. (U) Nielson interview, OH 20-86. (TS-CCO)
79. (U) Nielson interview, OH 20-86. (TS-CCO)
80. (U) GENS-14 Monthly Operation Summary, January 1957, Accession Number 10243, Cryptologic Archival Holding Area, NSA. (TSC ▮▮▮▮▮
81. (U) Nielson interview, OH 20-86. (TS-CCO)
82. (U) GENS-14 Monthly Operation Summary, March 1957, Accession Number 10243, Cryptologic Archival Holding Area, NSA. (TSC ▮▮▮▮▮
83. (U) GENS-44 Monthly Operational Summary, April 1957, Accession Number 10243, Cryptologic Archival Holding Area, NSA. (TSC ▮▮▮▮▮
84. (U) ▮▮▮▮▮ Intercept." (SC)
85. (U) GENS-44 Monthly Operational Summary, April 1957, Accession Number 10243, Cryptologic Archival Holding Area, NSA; GENS-44 Monthly Operational Summary, May 1957, Accession Number 10243, Cryptologic Archival Holding Area, NSA. (TSC ▮▮▮▮▮
86. (U) ▮▮▮▮▮ Intercept." (TSC)
87. (U) GENS-44 Monthly Operational Summary, May 1957, Accession Number 10243, Cryptologic Archival Holding Area, NSA. (TSC)
88. (U) Index of ▮▮▮▮▮ Soviet REGAL Summaries, 1 February 1957. (TSC)
89. (U) ▮▮▮▮▮ Rowlett, "Tunnel." (S)
90. (U) GENS-44 Monthly Operational Summary, September 1957, Accession Number 10243, Cryptologic Archival Holding Area, NSA. (TSC)
91. (U) Nielson interview, OH 20-86. (TS-CCO)

(b)(1)
(b)(3)
OGA

CIA

(b)(1)
(b)(3)-50 USC 403
(b)(3)-P.L. 86-36

(b)(1)
(b)(3)-P.L. 86-

(b)(1)
(b)(3)-P.L. 86-

(b)(1)
(b)(3)-P.L. 86-

92. (U) GENS-44 Monthly Operational Summary, November 1957, Accession Number 10243, Cryptologic Archival Holding Area, NSA. (TSC)

93. (U) GENS-44 Monthly Operational Summary, December 1957, Accession Number 10243, Cryptologic Archival Holding Area, NSA. (TSC)

94. (U) GENS-44 Monthly Operational Summary, January 1958, Accession Number 10243, Cryptologic Archival Holding Area, NSA. (TSC)

95. (U) One channel day represented a continuous piece of hard copy containing the traffic transmitted in one direction on one circuit for a 24-hour period.

96. (U) GENS-44 Monthly Operational Summary, December 1957, Accession Number 10243, Cryptologic Archival Holding Area, NSA. (TSC)

97. (U) GENS-44 Monthly Operational Summary, April 1958, Accession Number 10243, Cryptologic Archival holding Area, NSA. (TSC)

98. (U) GENS-44 Monthly Operational Summary, June 1958, Accession Number 10243, Cryptologic Archival Holding Area, NSA. (TSC)

99. (U) Nielson interview, OH 20-86. (TS-CCO)

100. (U) Dibben interview, OH 09-85. (TSC SENS/LIMDIS)

101. (U) [redacted] Rowlett, "Tunnel," Appendix A: *Discovery by the Soviets of PBJOINTLY*. (S)

102. (U) [redacted] Rowlett, "Tunnel," Appendix A. (S)

103. (U) [redacted] Rowlett, "Tunnel," Appendix A. (S)

104. (U) Martin, *Wilderness*, p. 87. (U)

105. (U) "Great Berlin Tunnel Mystery," *Life*, (7 May 1956) 40:48. (U)

106. (U) Walter Sullivan, "Russians Say U.S. Taps Berlin Wire: They Show Tunnel Allegedly Dug from West to Listen in on Eastern Phones," *The New York Times*, (24 April 1956) 1:5. (U)

107. (U) "East Germans File a Wiretap Protest," *The New York Times*, (26 April 1956) 1:5. (U)

108. (U) Sullivan, "Russians." (U)

109. (U) Cookridge, *George Blake*, p. 158. (U)

110. (U) Walter Sullivan, "U.S. Investigates Wiretap Tunnel: Aides in Berlin Say They Are Looking into Soviet Charge of Phone Espionage," *The New York Times*, (25 April 1956) 8:3. (U)

111. (C) According to an NSA engineer stationed in Berlin at the time [redacted] See Interview [redacted] 17 July 1986 by Robert D. Farley and Thomas Johnson, OH 19-86, NSA. (TS)

112. (U) Sullivan, "Russians." (U)

113. (U) Martin, *Wilderness*, p. 87. (U)

114. (U) "Reds Play Up Berlin Tunnel," *The New York Times*, (29 April 1956) 29:3. (U)

115. (U) "Reds Blame Dulles' Sister," *The New York Times*, (11 May 1956) 2:6 (U)

116. (U) Martin, *Wilderness*, p. 87. (U)

117. (U) [redacted] Rowlett, "Tunnel." (S)

118. (U) Interview Frank B. Rowlett, 14 May 1985, by Robert D. Farley, Henry Schorreck, and Gerald K. Haines, OH 10-85, NSA. (S-CCO)

119. (U) Cookridge, *George Blake*. (U)

120. (U) Seth S. King, "Briton Sentenced as Spy for Soviet," *The New York Times*, (4 May 1961) 1:8. (U)

121. (U) "Ex-British Aide Held on Security Charge," *The New York Times*, (19 April 1961) 16:6. (U)

122. (U) "Briton Accused as Spy," *The New York Times*, (25 April 1961) 3:6. (U)

123. (U) Martin, *Wilderness*, p. 100. George Blake served time in Wormwood Scrubs Prison. Although originally placed on the escape list and allocated a special security cell, the "model prisoner" was removed from this list in October 1961. He escaped from prison on 22 October 1966 with the help of fellow prisoner Sean Alphonsus Bourke of the Irish Republican Army. They arrived in Moscow several weeks later, where Blake was awarded the Order of Lenin. For more information see Sean Bourke, *The Springing of George Blake* (New York: The Viking Press, Inc., 1970), and E. H. Cookridge, *The Many Sides of George Blake Esq.* (Princeton: Brandon/Systems Press, Inc., 1970). (U)

124. (U) "Spy Had No U.S. Data," *The New York Times*, (6 May 1961) 22:6. (U)

125. (U) Rowlett interview, OH 10-85. (S-CCO)

126. (U) Martin, *Wilderness*, p. 100. According to Sean Bourke, Blake boasted that "the KGB knew about the tunnel before the first spadeful of earth was dug out of the ground. I saw to that." See Bourke, *The Springing of George Blake*, p. 275. This account has not been substantiated. (U)

127. (U) Martin, *Wilderness*, p. 101. (U)

128. [redacted] See [redacted] interview, OH 19-86. (TS)

129. (U) Of perhaps minor significance to the compromise of the tunnel was the presence of Kim Philby who defected in 1963, confirming his involvement in spy activities first suspected in 1951 with the defections of Donald Maclean and Guy Burgess. Philby had been the MI-6 representative in Washington in 1949, serving as a liaison between the U.S. and U.K. intelligence organizations. Although he remained in British intelligence until 1963, he was under sufficient suspicion to limit his access to certain sensitive materials. Although it is quite probable that he had some knowledge of the existence of [redacted] via official or unofficial channels, he did not mention the Berlin tunnel in the autobiography he later published from Moscow. (U)

130. (U) Dibben interview, OH 09-85. (TSC SENS/LIMDIS)
131. (U) Allen Dulles, *The Craft of Intelligence* (New York: Harper and Row, Publishers, 1963), pp. 206–7. (U)
132. (U) Nielson interview, OH 20-86. (TS-CCO)
133. (U) Martin, *Wilderness*, p. 88. (U)
134. (U) Nielson interview, OH 20-86. (TS-CCO)
135. (U) ☐ Intercept." (TSC)
136. (U) ☐ Rowlett, "Tunnel," Appendix B: *Recapitulation of the Intelligence Derived.* (S)
137. (U) ☐ Rowlett, "Tunnel," Appendix B: *Recapitulation of the Intelligence Derived.* (S)
138. (U) The CIA later obtained additional information concerning Zhukov's fall from power from Oleg Penkovskiy, a Soviet defector who had served as a high-ranking member of Soviet military intelligence. See Oleg Penkovskiy, *The Penkovskiy Papers*, trans. Peter Deriabin, with an introduction by Frank Gibney (New York: Ballantine Books, 1982). (U)
139. (U) ☐ Rowlett, "Tunnel," Appendix B: *Recapitulation.* (S)
140. (U) ☐
141. (U) ☐ Rowlett, "Tunnel." (S)
142. (U) ☐ Rowlett, "Tunnel." (S)
143. (U) ☐ Rowlett, "Tunnel." (S)
144. (U) ☐ iew, OH 20-86. (TS-CCO)
145. (U) ☐ Rowlett, "Tunnel." (S)
146. (U) GENS-143 Monthly Operational Summary, December 1956, Accession Number 10243, Cryptologic Archival Holding Area, NSA. (TSC ☐ (S)
147. (U) ☐ Rowlett, "Tunnel." (S)

(b)(1)
(b)(3)
OGA

(b)(1)
(b)(3)-50 USC 403
(b)(3)-P.L. 86-36

(b)(3)-P.L. 86-36
(b)(1)
(b)(3)-50 USC 403
(b)(3)-18 USC 798

(b)(1)
(b)(3)-P.L. 86-36

www.ingramcontent.com/pod-product-compliance
Lightning Source LLC
Chambersburg PA
CBHW060443060326
40690CB00019B/4320